DEAR YOUNG KINGS AND QUEENS

A Book of Affirmations for the Transitioning Youth

SHANOVIA LUMPKIN

Published by True Beginnings Publishing.
Copyright by Shanovia Lumpkin, 2019.

Dear Young Kings and Queens, by Shanovia Lumpkin. © Copyright 2019. All Rights Reserved and Preserved. No part of this book may be reproduced or transmitted in any form or by any means, electronic or mechanical, including photocopying, recording, or by information storage and retrieval systems or other electronic or mechanical methods, without written permission of the Author with exceptions as to brief quotes, references, articles, reviews and certain other noncommercial uses permitted by copyright law. For permission requests, write to the Publisher, addressed "Attention: Permissions," at the address below.

true_beginnings_publishing@yahoo.com

Formatting, Editing, and all artwork by True Beginnings Publishing. All Illustrations, Cover Art, and text are Copyright Protected.

ISBN-13: 978-1-947082-70-0
ISBN-10: 1-947082-70-1

Ordering Information:
To order additional copies of this book, please visit Amazon or the Author's website at: https://priceless-treasures.org/

This book is a compilation of affirmations by the Author. All quotes, thoughts, and writings are products of the Author's imagination. Any resemblance to actual events or persons, living or dead, is entirely coincidental. The quotes, thoughts, and writings are copyrighted to the Author and are protected under US Copyright law. Any theft of the Author's work will be prosecuted to the full extent of the law.

Dear Young Kings and Queens.
© Shanovia Lumpkin.
First Printing, 2019.

~Dedication~

To every young man and woman
on a search to find their identity.
Use this as a guide to light your way
and mold you into the individual
you are destined to be.

~**Scripture/Quote**~

Make intelligent decisions.
Speak Less, Listen More, and Stay Focused.
-Shanovia Lumpkin

~Introduction~

I know what it's like to be a struggling youth, trying to live up to everyone's expectations, all while facing daily adversity. It is so hard trying to be everything to everyone and still maintain your own identity.

Growing up I saw, heard, and experienced so much. I had parents who told me what to do (parental advisement), society providing the image I should reflect (social media is telling you what is accepted), teachers paid to tell me what I should learn (academic education), churches telling me what I should believe (religion), peer pressure and influence from friends (anxiety and acceptance), body changing (puberty), life (unpredictable), mental overload (I need peace of mind).

I was constantly questioning: Who am I? It took a while, but I realized I am the master of my own fate. No matter what I was taught or told, I controlled the outcome. It was up to me to implement my teachings into my everyday life.

Between the tender age of 8-18, we tend to go through so many transitions. When I began writing this book, it was initially for my children and later evolved into a book for all transitioning youth. My goal is to reach a multitude of youth, providing them with daily affirmations to promote positive thinking, confidence, empathy, and compassion.

For every youth that cried out for help, craved love, wanted attention, and was open to guidance, I created this for you. This is a guide to help you along the way. It's about what works for you. No matter how long the path may be, stay the course and see it through.

Dear young Kings and Queens, what you think and how you feel will determine what you will become. Get in the habit of waking up every day and affirming yourself. Speak life, love, hope, change, prosperity, and peace. Know that there is nothing that you can't handle. Feed the next generation knowledge to make our youth a better version of people.

~Guidance~

Create your own happiness.
Do not allow anything or anyone to steal your joy.
You have too much to be thankful for.
You are the master of your fate.
The captain of your ship.
The director of your film.
The life you live is up to you.

-Shanovia Lumpkin

~Hers/His/Theirs~

You are Kings and Queens, descended from royalty, strength, and love. Let your actions speak volumes to the next generation to come.

I can do all things through Christ
who gives me strength.
Today, I will be productive
and proactive.
I will remain focused and
accomplish the many goals I've set
for myself.
I will not be distracted.
I am focused.
I am prepared.
I vow to finish what I start, from
beginning to end.

When you speak, let it reflect your character. Learn to communicate effectively. Be cautious and aware of your word choice, dialect, and the context in which you use them. Be mindful of your tone and body language. The worst thing you could do is offend someone intentionally or unintentional. It is so easy to offend someone when you are not mindful of the words that come out of your mouth, how you say them, and the body language you use when speaking.

Shanovia Lumpkin

Ignore the ignorant!
Do not stoop to their level.
Never mimic their ways.
Maintain your position.
Let your actions speak louder than your words.
Stop procrastinating, take hold of your life, and walk into your purpose.
You are extraordinary.
You are destined for greatness.
You are blessed.

The only person you should be in competition with is yourself. Stop looking for validation and learn to validate yourself. I've learned when you leave that power in the hands of others, you allow their thoughts and opinions to make or break you. Don't set yourself up for failure. Critique yourself, correct yourself, and make the necessary changes to be a better you.

No one is perfect.
My theory is anyone who is diligently working towards bettering themselves, accepting fault, and correcting their ways and/or bad habits are perfection in progress.
You are perfection in progress.

Protect your heart, mind, body, and spirit. The fate of your humanity rests upon it. Know that broken promises lead to broken trust. Words are just words if you never see effort. See the truth in one's actions and take heed.

Shanovia Lumpkin

It's okay to disconnect yourself from anything or anyone that isn't good for your self-growth.
If it has more complaints, compared to compliments or praise, let it go.
It may be hard, but you can do it.
Step out on faith and trust God.

Negative thoughts and toxic memories can be the death of one's spirit. We must learn to fill our mind, spirit, and body with positive energy.
Pray and meditate.
Be mindful of who and what you surround yourself with.
It all plays a role in your growth.

Shanovia Lumpkin

They don't know you! They are only looking at the outer shell. Only the real will take the time to get to know the real you, your heart, mind, body, and spirit. It takes a special and patient person to learn every layer of you. Be patient.

Never allow your feelings to cloud your better judgement. Your feelings can sometimes act as a smoke screen that blocks the truth. Don't allow it to make you comfortable with living in a fantasy. Be mentally strong, be firm in your actions, and focus on the bigger picture.

Shanovia Lumpkin

Less emoji's, more words.
Your voice is one of the most
powerful tools you possess.
Remove the invisible muzzle and
speak your truth. If you can master
the art of verbal communication and
articulation, you can unlock many
opportunities in life.

No day will be perfect, but make the best of every moment!
Be a team player!
You must give a little to get a little.
What you sow is what you shall reap.
We all need somebody sometimes, so don't burn bridges.

Giving up is not an option. We all get knocked down every so often.
That's life.
Get up, dust yourself off, and keep on pushing. Keep on trying. Keep on praying. Keep on striving, and keep on believing. You are greatness in motion. Consistency is key. Never get complacent or comfortable because you are so much more than this modern-day mediocracy.

Dear Young Kings and Queens

Learn to be grateful and appreciative. Gratitude and appreciation go a long way. Kind gestures currently do not come often, so be thankful when you are blessed with even the smallest tokens of love.

Train your mind to never speak negatively of someone else. Ask yourself what you are to gain from slandering someone's name. Encourage yourself to be a mute when you have nothing positive to say. Silence can be the best tool of defense and retaliation. It's okay to be the bigger person.

It is time to start believing in yourself. You must remember how intelligent you are, how talented you are. Push yourself the way you push others. Pray as hard for yourself as you do others. Let your uniqueness separate you from the norm. Sometimes, you must do something you've never done to accomplish something you thought wasn't possible. Step out on faith and be exactly what you've always been, GREATNESS.

Take hold of your life. If you want better, you must do better. When you change your surroundings and mindset, then you will see a change in your situation.

Be mindful of your behavior, be watchful of your surroundings, and be cautious about every life decision. Speak less, listen more, and stay focused.

Knowledge is everything. Feed your mind, body, and spirit with fruits of growth. Inhale everything that makes you better. Eliminate and block out anything that is toxic. Clear your mentality and purify your heart. Free yourself of anything that will stunt your growth.

Shanovia Lumpkin

We are very emotional creatures, and honestly, we sometimes set ourselves up, wanting and expecting things from people that are not where we are or want what we want mentally, spiritually, physically, and emotionally. That's why we must be clear what things are before we just drop our guard and become completely vulnerable to uncertain situations.

You are amazing, hand-designed by God. You are perfect in an imperfect world. You have a purpose. Your birth was not in vain, and your existence isn't for naught. No matter what life throws at you, you must stay focused. Love yourself and walk in your Destiny.

Stop attaching yourself to people and things that are not ordained by God. If it is not in God's plans for you, it will not prosper.

Shanovia Lumpkin

Never be silent about things that bother you. Address them head on. Be clear and use a calm voice. Aggressive body language and tone will get you nothing but an escalated situation with zero results. It's not what you say but how you say and approach any situation.

Rumors and gossip are traits of the weak! What does it profit you to listen or spread the business of others? Most rumors are lies and accusation in heavy rotation. Ask yourself what do you have to gain? Be the one that has more important things to do than to entertain sweet nothings.

There is always room to bloom.
Even the most minute of change for the better is progress.
Complacency is the root of normality and underachievers.
Therefore, one should always strive to be their best self.
See the greatness within yourself and never settle for anything other than what you deserve.
You're priceless. Never forget that.

We all have things that we struggle with. Let's be honest, no one is perfect. All we can do is take things one day at a time through baby steps, because we all had to crawl before we walked. Patience and prayer will get you through. A sound mind and determination will assist in your change, and believing in your progress will be your overall success. Just hold on.
Everything will be alright.

Pay attention to the signs.
Not everything that feels good to you is good for you. If you find yourself questioning more than you are just enjoying, it is time for a change.
If it does not make you better as a person, then let it go.
When in doubt, leave it out of your life. Some things are just here for a season, but we tend to try and hold on for a lifetime. Accept that some things are not meant to be, only a lesson you needed to learn. Embrace the knowledge, take it in stride, and keep moving forward. There are greater things ahead patiently waiting on you.

Say what you mean and mean what you say. Think before you speak. Don't just be talking because you like the sound of your own voice. Let your words mean something, and let your actions reflect your words.

Don't get distracted.
Don't get lazy.
Stay focused.
You're almost there!
So many expect you to fail.
Make success and perseverance your daily state of mind. Remember, you can do all things through Christ who gives you strength.

Stop looking to be perfect
in a world of imperfection.
Stop living to impress and please
others, but instead, live your life
unapologetically as you please with
no restrictions. Understand that if
you allow others to dictate your life
and live theirs, you are the one who
will forever be unhappy.

Control your temper and channel your anger. Know that you will always be tested, but you must be stronger than your emotions. It's okay to use your brain over your brawn. It may just save you from an even worse situation.

We all have a purpose.
Identify with yours and be the rarest being the world has ever seen.
Mark my words, you will be one of the greats, if not the greatest!
Speak less, listen more, stay focused, put in the work, and make intelligent decisions. Everything your heart desires will be yours.

No regrets, only lessons learned! My focus is to remain focused and reach all my goals.
I will not live in the past.
I will work towards my future.
I will continue to pray and stick to my plans with no distractions and no doubts. I can do all things through Christ who gives me strength.

Dedicate today to
the improvement of yourself!
Improve your attitude.
Improve your mindset.
Improve your generosity.
Improve your love.
Change is good, and progress is
great. Shake up your environment
with change.

Shanovia Lumpkin

I wish I could give you my eyes so you can see the greatness I see in you. Be yourself! Do not allow anything or anyone to make you feel like you are not good enough. What you think, what you feel, and the way you carry yourself determines your value.
You are enough!

Calm your spirit.
Breathe in deeply.
Exhale slowly.
Do not allow every little thing to upset and aggravate you.
Control your mood.
Anchor your day.
Create a euphoric space of peace so dominant it radiates onto everyone around you.

Be thankful for what you have!
So many forget how to appreciate
and be grateful for the many
treasures in life as they try to keep up
with society. Live within your means
until your time comes. Prioritize,
organize, and execute.
Most downfalls come from the lack
of planning.

Giving up is not an option. There are too many depending on you. You must show them what strong is. It's okay to nurture and love unconditionally. Never show the pain or the struggle, just your strength and love. It won't be easy, but it's necessary. I'm praying for you. Everything will work out for you, no worries. Just move smart from here on out.

Telling someone you are sorry for how you wronged them is acknowledgement, but until you back it up with improvement in your actions, they are just words. Appreciate people today. Don't wait until it's too late to start showing value in one's presence.

Visualize your success!
Let nothing and no one steer you away from the goal/goals you are trying to reach. Distractions are a hindrance to someone with a purpose. Be steadfast and focused, for the light at the end of the tunnel is greater than the temporary fixes along the way.

Shanovia Lumpkin

Find your strength, even in the pain.
Keep pushing forward.
Never show weakness.
Success is your goal, and failure is not an option.
It's time to stand on your own.
You can never grow if you continue to be dependent on others.
Following season is over.
It's time to lead.

Reciprocation and appreciation go a long way. Don't be the friend that is always in need and never gives. Let your actions and words express appreciation. If the giving, compromise, and sacrifices are one-sided, there can never be balance.

Shanovia Lumpkin

So many walk in fear,
afraid to make mistakes,
afraid to take risks,
and afraid to fail.
But one thing I've learned is
there's nothing wrong with stepping
out on faith.
Learn from your mistakes.
Try!
Because even if you fail, you can get
back up and try again.
I thank God for my lessons. They
only motivated me to want more, do
more, and be more.
#noregretsonlylessonslearned

Thank God for the process!
It leads you to the progress.
Blood, sweat, and tears.
Distractions and disappointments
may come, but stay the course and
believe you've already won.

Shanovia Lumpkin

Want more for yourself.
Never get content or complacent in the now, but strive for a better future. You deserve it, you must want it, and you must be willing to put in the work. Get in the Nike state of mind and Just Do It.

You must be clear, precise, and direct with every area of your life. Leave no room for misunderstandings or mistakes. Perfect your communication skills. Effective communication is the most important tool needed for a productive life.

Not everyone deserves the title of friend. There are so many that surround you that are wolves in sheep's clothing, patiently waiting on your downfall. People who smile in your face but harbor ill feelings for you in their heart. Ones who hide envy and jealously behind sarcasm. Be watchful and cautious of the one who never likes to see you happy, doing good, and making progress. Downsize your circle. These people are called frenemies, not friends.

Today is a new day,
another day of life and opportunity.
Don't waste it, get up, get out, and do something productive.
You can never evolve while being complacent. You can never grow if you're not feeding your heart, mind, body, and spirit.
You must be hungry!
Not just for food, but for knowledge, for stability, and for life. Don't get lost in the shuffle. You have to be the deck. Start building your foundation, but make sure it's on solid ground.

Stay humble, no matter what.
Never allow anything or anyone to bring you out of character.
No one should have that much power over you.
No one.

Forgiveness is key in everyday life.
No one is perfect.
We were all born in sin, shaped in iniquity. There is no perfect human.
We all make mistakes.
We all fall short, but the goal is to try your hardest not to make the same mistake again. Just to simply try to be better than yesterday is progress.
One day at a time.
One goal at a time.
One success at a time.

Shanovia Lumpkin

Don't lose focus.
Depend on yourself.
Strengthen your mind.
Take care of your body, and keep the faith. Take life one day at a time.

We all fall short sometimes, but we get up and try our best not to fall again. No one is perfect, so understand that you are still a work in progress. Stay humble, no matter what. Never allow anyone to bring you out of character.

Never accept defeat.
No matter how many times you fall, pick yourself up, dust yourself off, and keep trying.
Keep giving your all.
It will pay off in due time.

You can't change people; you can only change how you deal with them. You never know what people are going through or how they view themselves. Just know that someone admires and look up to you. No matter what life throws at you, you will endure it and continue to persevere. Accomplish your goals and continue to be humble. Your humility will always make you cautious of your actions, and your actions reflect your character, so be the role model that you seek. Be the reflection of positive energy and growth.

Move in silence.
Ask God to remove anything and everything in your life that is toxic for your progression.
Set goals and stay focused.
Trust me, it will not be easy.
You will be tempted.
You will be tested.
There will be trials, but you must be adamant about bettering yourself and your surroundings.
Don't fret.
Just be prayerful and patient.
Everything will work itself out.

Actions speak louder than words, so today, let your actions reflect your words. Be proactive, be productive, and be diligent. Be dedicated. Make an effort for better results.

Giving up is never an option.
I know your body is tired, and the lack of sleep doesn't make it any better, but you have responsibilities, priorities, and goals.
No matter what, keep pushing, keep praying, and keep believing.
The end results will be worth it.
Trust that the fruits of your labor will not be in vain.

Individuals stand out!
When you are confident in your uniqueness, there is nothing and no one that can dim your light. Love the skin that you are in because it was created just for you.
Be unapologetically you! Bold, brave, and different. Never be ashamed of who you are! You were never meant to blend in, just humbly shine in every setting. Learn to embrace all of you, and be proud of the dynamic person you are.
These are all the qualities that makes you special.

You do not need an entourage, nor do you need validation to define who you are. You define who you are. Never allow the thoughts and opinions of others to deter you from fulfilling your divine purpose.
You are the anchor of your life. Everyone else is just sightseeing.

Shanovia Lumpkin

There are things in life we have no control over. All we can do is pray.
What's meant to be will be.
What's not meant will be another experience, a memory, and a lesson.
Take it in stride, keep your head up, and keep moving forward.
#nopainnogain

Dear Young Kings and Queens

You are Kings and Queens, descended from royalty, strength, and love. Let your actions speak volumes to the next generation to come.

~**Acknowledgements**~

I would like to thank God for my many lessons and blessings. In everything I do, I will always acknowledge you. Through all my life's transitions, you never left my side, and for that I am grateful.

To my sons Jeremiah, Devin Jr., and Zhyon: you are my John 14:6. I call you The Way, The Truth, and The Life. You taught me strength, patience, and resilience. To my daughter Journee: you are my Psalms 37:4. You are what my heart desired. You are the blessing after the storm. At that time in my life, God knew I needed a silver lining. You are the softer side of me. Together, you guys gave love a new meaning.

To Germaine. Thank you for always pushing me to strive for more. You will forever be my innovative partner in crime.

To Brenda Westbrook. I would like to thank you for all that you've done and all that you do. You are appreciated.

To Frances Magdaleno and Devin Tullis, my print preview. Thank you for being patient and open to listen to my words prior to publishing. I appreciate you.

My Priceless Treasures: Tremiah Wilson, Breanna Westbrook, Arieana Chipman, Breanna Mitchell, Lashawn Travis, Donnicia Walker, Yakiyah Mala, Brianna Berrain, Alanah Rose, Daphney Alexis, Nialah Lumpkin, and Danaisha Dove. Distractions come in all forms. Stay focused and make intelligent decisions. Remember, you are a priceless treasure, rare, beautiful, and blessed. Know your worth always and never settle.

My Young Men of Standard: Javaughn Salesman, Jabari Maddox, Jahnoi Salesman, Assan Salesman, Javin Simpkins, Bobby Jackson III, Dwayne Lowe III, Devon Sutton Jr., Trevante Allen, Larod Caldwell, Kendrick Williams, Donald Burch Jr., Debon Brown, Kristian Stanley, Treyvonn Charles, and Ibram Alexander Jr. Nothing in life will come easy, but through hard work and focus you can achieve any and everything set in your mind to do. Young Kings, you are loved, needed, wanted, and appreciated.

To the Girls of Pearls of Sun Rise High School: Rayven Tobin, Keytiana Smith, Paizlii Brinson, Kayla Herrington, Anitra Singletary, Bianca Joseph, Jada Matthews, Kira Williams, Jamerah Walker, Kivanni Rollins, Daniella Jeanty, and Jedeline Nicolas. Thank you for being a part of this journey. Meeting you all was an amazing experience. We laughed, we cried, we reflected, dissected, and created plans to be better. I am glad I was a part of your positive transition.

My Wee Ones: Da'Mya Scrivens, Zuri Parks, Jynesis Eloi, Juelz Eloi, Kennedy Coleman, Delon Coleman, Deiondra Coleman, Trenajah Wilson, Treliyah Wilson, Tremeyah Wilson, Trekeyah Wilson, Elijah Wiley, Kenneth Phillips Jr., Kason Phillips, Ezra Wiley, Dmari Cadeau, Aundre Taylor, Annettie McKinsey, Jannetta McKinsey, Danae'sha Jackson, Zion Jackson, Li'aishia Jackson, Ja'marie Edwards, Jamayah Edwards, Joanna Edwards, Cedrick Martin Jr., Cameron Beacham, Dorian Randle, Dezrea Cearnel, Fall Strachan, Issac Harris Jr., Imani Cearnel, Jahnine Laguerre, Jordyn Duroseau, Joshua Washington Jr., Jayden Washington, Janari Washington, Jehan Taylor, Jamir Washington, Kassidy Rodgers, Lailani Caldwell, Lamar Atkins Jr., Lemmari Jones, Lerio Mennis, Meliah Rose Duroseau, Maliah Kay Duroseau, Makaiyah Burch, N'Deirah Case, Nila Holmes, Shonterria Smith, Shoniylah Amores, Payton Williams, Tah'Siah Case, N'Deirah Case, Jahnine Laguerre, Nila Holmes, Meliah Rose Duroseau, Maliah Kay Duroseau, Jehan Taylor, Ibram Alexander, Makaiyah Burch, Amiyah Mala, Ahyana Mala,

Lamar Atkins Jr., Tyhanna Wiley, Tytiana Wiley, Kassidy Rodgers, Jordyn Duroseau, Shonterria Smith, Shoniylah Amores, Carter King Farquharson, Cateleya Charles, Le'brian Charles, Lemmari Jones, Corey Lumpkin Jr., Delman Lumpkin Jr., Ayanni Forestal, Ayden Lee, Tre'Shaud Nottage, Makylee Adams, Nasir Kusi, Amani Kusi, Zeus Randle, Armani Salley Janise Hargrove Michael Hargrove Jr., and Kamari Knowles. You are all amazing. You were not created to blend in but always stand out. You are a gift that keeps on giving. So, continue to shine! No matter what, keep pushing, keep praying, and never give up. Your season is coming.

~About The Author~

Shanovia Lumpkin, also known as Priceless Treasure, is a freelance writer born and raised in Miami Florida where she learned the value of an education at a very young age. As a graduate from Miami Norland Senior High School, Shanovia developed a keen interest in expressive writing, which became evident in the eloquence of her poetry.

It was then that Priceless Treasure found her inner strength and self-awareness that propelled her into a life of abundance through vigilant affirmations and prayer.

"Priceless Treasures" is her first published book.

You can also find the Author in these places:

~**Website**~ ~**Twitter**~ ~**Instagram**~
priceless-treasures.org @PricelessT21588 _pricelesstreasures

~**Email**~ ~**Tumblr**~
shanovianicole@gmail.com priceless-treasures.tumblr.com

~**Facebook**~
www.facebook.com/PricelessTreasuresShanoviaLumpkin

www.ingramcontent.com/pod-product-compliance
Lightning Source LLC
Chambersburg PA
CBHW070102100426
42743CB00012B/2634